Punch YOUR FEAR in the Face

Discovering Your Purpose and Conquering Your Fears

LaShana Gardner

TABLE OF CONTENTS

DEDICATION

Barbara (My mommy),

Your strength, your courage, and your love have shaped me into the woman that I am today. I am forever grateful for all the wisdom you have given me. Thank you for always encouraging me to go after my dreams and for believing in me! You are such a blessing and I love you more than words could ever express!

Tamara and RaSheeda (My sisters),

Thank you both for always protecting me and for watching over me. You have been my biggest cheerleaders and supporters and you have always had my back. You are my angels on this earth. Thanks for loving me! I love you both SO much!

Asheley (My very best friend),

Thank you for being one of my angels on this earth. You are the kind of best friend that everyone should have. Thank you for always praying with me, believing in me, being honest with me, and for simply being you. I love you!

To all the dreamers,

NEVER STOP DREAMING BIG! You have something inside of you that this world needs and I wrote this book to help you discover the true gift that you are! Get ready to let go of fear, step out on faith, and go after the life you truly desire.

INTRODUCTION

Hi, my friends,

I pray that each and every one of you reading this book gains valuable insight that will push you forward and assist you with learning how to not allow fear to cripple you. Fear can cripple you when you allow fearful thoughts to stop you from taking action. However, taking action even when you do not know the outcome will bring you results.

You might tell yourself that you will start when the time is just right. I am here to tell you that the time will never be just right. You must trust the journey and simply jump. When those thoughts of fear tell you all the reasons why it may not work out, you must shift your attention and place your focus on ways to make it work. YOU are the only person who can make your dreams come true!

In this book, I am going to show you how you can take control and decide that every day you are alive is another opportunity to fulfill your God-given purpose on this earth. You can decide today that you will not be on your deathbed full of dreams unfulfilled. You can choose to leave your footprints on this earth and grow old without regrets by giving this life your all. This world needs the gifts that the Lord placed on the inside of you.

I wrote this book for those that are ready to birth their visions and live out their true passions. If that is you, then *Punch Your Fear In The Face* will become your new best friend and guide. It will help you discover what is truly stopping you. Are you ready to take the leap? If so, then the following pages await you! Enjoy!

CHAPTER ONE

❦

The Power of Your Mind and Mouth

You are a WINNER! Yes, YOU reading this book! The question is, do you believe that? What you think and what you say to yourself have more influence over your life than you can fathom. Your beliefs are SO powerful and if you are not where you want to be in life just yet, then your harmful thinking patterns could be the reason why.

Many people go day-to-day saying the most negative things to themselves while wondering why they feel so lousy. They feel lousy because they speak lousily. Therefore, you must choose your thoughts and words with care. Thinking positive on purpose and taking control of your thinking are just as important as choosing what you wear or eat each day. Learn to carry yourself like you have already won and are living the life you desire.

Imagine what it would feel like to accomplish that goal you have been working toward. Would you feel joyous, full of energy, and ready to take on each day? Would you be proud of how far you have come? Would you be appreciative of your blessings? Write out a full page of the person you envision yourself being in the future. How do you dress, where do you go, how do you speak, where do you live, and who do you hang out with? Write out as many details as possible. Once you visualize who you want to become, that is where you should place your attention daily, not on defeat.

Become full of the feeling you would have if you were currently living in the world as the person you envision yourself being in the future. Shift your anxious thinking and ask yourself, "What if everything works out in my favor?" Then continue to place your attention on the results of your hard work. This positive mindset will help you create positive circumstances. Whatever YOU focus on will amplify in your life. If you are constantly focusing on uplifting yourself, focusing on the good, telling yourself you are a winner, and choosing to be happy on purpose, then more of that will be brought forth in your life.

I am not speaking on "name it, claim it". I am speaking on choosing from your inner being to be in a state of happiness, resting in God's perfect timing, and choosing to have a good outlook on your life. Be a cheerful voice in your life's journey. You are LISTENING to you, so if you are always speaking defeat, then how do you think that will make you feel? You cannot feel amazing when you are always word bashing, name-calling, flaw picking, and tearing yourself apart. Just think about how it feels when a stranger or someone close to you calls you a bad name or constantly brings up a negative experience from your past. It does not make you feel like a winner does it?

Instead, it makes you feel bad and causes you to focus on things that are not enhancing you as a person. It is time for YOU to see yourself how God sees you, as a beautiful masterpiece. You are amazing, you are unique, you are talented, you are loved, you are creative, you are enough, you are worth it, you are a shining star, and you are a blessing!

Now how good did being encouraged feel? You must learn to encourage yourself, to pat yourself on the back, and to tell yourself that no matter how much you may have screwed up in the past, or how much defeat you have spoken over your life, you can declare today that you will have the victory and come out on top. Just as you should consume nourishing foods, you also should consume positive thoughts to nourish your mind and your soul on a daily basis.

Look at your mind as a garden. What you constantly plant in your garden will grow in your life. When those weeds attempt to grow in the form of a negative thought, pluck it immediately. Keep planting beautiful seeds inside of your garden, and watering those seeds with daily encouraging self-talks, and eventually, you will see a beautiful harvest.

Write down ten compliments about yourself, ten reasons why you are a winner, and ten reasons why you believe in yourself. Re-read this list when you find yourself in a mental funk. To become a master of your own mind and thinking, repeat the following several times a day: "I AM A WINNER", "I CAN DO IT", "I HAVE THE VICTORY".

Learning how to gain control of your mind is one of the best things you could ever do for yourself. It takes time and persistent work. The mind will naturally drift into "Negative Nancy" land unless you learn to control your thoughts. The mind will naturally reflect on everything that is wrong or what you should or should not have done and drift into the "poor me, why me" space. Do not allow your thoughts to run rampant. Do not allow your thoughts to control you.

Learn to cast down those crazy thoughts immediately and allow your mind to submit to positive thinking.

This might be difficult to do when you first start analyzing your thoughts. You will be amazed at just how negative you sometimes think. It will seem like your thoughts are at war with you, causing you to focus on what is going wrong instead of what is going right in your life. Whenever I am in a funky mood, it is usually because I have allowed my mind to drift into that "poor me" space. I have learned to catch my crazy thoughts, however. I will say out loud, "No, I am not going to focus on that," then I replace my negative thought with a positive one. I will start to give thanks for any and everything that I can think of. I will ask myself, "What can I learn from this situation that's bothering me?" This allows my mind to shift from focusing on the problem to finding solutions and to being grateful for the good things in my life. I am still working on this area, too. Mental mastery takes time because you are literally learning to retrain your mind to think properly and teaching yourself what to think about. It is like putting yourself on a mental diet and feeding your mind the right, nurturing, positive mental food.

This practice became a crucial part of helping me with consciously choosing the right thought patterns. My mental food consists of positive books, the Bible, worship music, inspirational lectures, and surrounding myself with the right people. It is similar to training a muscle at the gym: you have to keep working on it to build it up. You have to consciously pay attention to your thoughts throughout the day and toss out the ones that do not benefit you. Do not beat yourself up when you have one of those days where you seem to think about all the wrong things. You are human and sometimes you will need to process those situations in your life, but do not let those days control you. Feel the annoyance then let it go.

Life happens to us all, and it is not always a fairy tale. I have experienced many hardships; I have wanted to quit. Instead of allowing those hard moments to keep me in a negative state, I took control of my mind. While growing my company, I have had to battle with self-doubt. I have experienced many moments of not knowing if I was good enough because I did not come from a background of entrepreneurs. I am the first person in my family to grow and start a business from scratch with absolutely no mentor.

My mom was a single parent and worked two to three jobs to make ends meet. I have always admired her strength and her determination taught me that if I wanted success, then I needed to work hard to get it. I was not born with a silver spoon in my mouth. *Pshhh*, I wish, as I am sure we all do at times. I have not had anything handed to me, so I speak from personal experience when I say life is not a fairy tale. I grew up in poverty. Therefore, I know what it is like to barely have enough money to cover the bills and still attempt to walk by faith. I know what it is like to have to budget every single penny. Nevertheless, I have not allowed those hard times to stop me.

At times entrepreneurship can make you feel like you are on an up and down, emotional roller coaster. Some days are great and other days are difficult. It has been a mental struggle for me at times because I have had thoughts like, "What if it doesn't work out?" or "What's my Plan B?" I am learning daily how to handle the rough patches. Is it always easy to control those thoughts of doubt? No, but I choose to push past it. I have learned to trust God with my tomorrows, to walk by faith, and to appreciate my progress. Sometimes you are going to have to cheer yourself up by placing your focus on the good, by putting your faith to work, by grinding it out even when you do not see any results, and by pushing yourself to keep pursuing it every day. It is my prayer that I am building a company that will be able to offer employment in the future.

Although I have battled with walking by faith when the journey gets tough, I know that I am growing something much bigger than me. It has made me a stronger, more resilient person. I am becoming someone I never knew existed all because I have chosen to activate my faith, cast down my fears, and take a different path. I decided that I would learn from every bump in the road and use those experiences to shape me into a better person. You must do the same.

Remember, negative thinking is a bad habit that you are attempting to break, and it will take daily work to retrain your brain. Negative thinking can become an obsession if the pattern is not interrupted and broken. It is easy to fall into the practice of imagining the worst-case scenario, or of constantly replaying a difficult experience. Do you ever find yourself thinking about the most negative thing that could happen? Do you always search for the worst in other people? Or do you find yourself constantly replaying a bad experience from your past? The subconscious mind is like a storehouse. It stores and retrieves data from your past; all of your memories, beliefs, and life experiences are programmed inside of your subconscious mind. It is from your memories that your habits and beliefs are formed. Your subconscious mind is subjective and obeys the commands from your conscious reasoning mind; therefore, it can be changed by what you choose to focus on.

Make some time each day, even if only for fifteen minutes, to lie down and relax. During your daily relaxation, repeat five or ten positive messages to yourself. Let's say you are dealing with an illness. Your positive message could be, "Regardless of what I currently see or feel, I am trusting God for complete restoration and healing in my body." Starting today, I encourage you to feed your mind positivity and to focus on that which uplifts you.

What you say to yourself, about yourself, matters. Your words will affect your life more than the words that anyone else might say to you or about you. Your mind is always listening to what you say both inwardly and outwardly. It is super important to use your words to build, uplift and encourage yourself, instead of using your words to knock yourself down.

Remember, you are human and you will make some mistakes. You must be kind and loving toward yourself. You must become your own best friend. Look in the mirror daily, smile, and speak words that will heal and calm your mind, instead of using words that only will make you anxious, worried and frustrated.

9

Tell yourself how proud of yourself you are for everything that you have accomplished thus far. Tell yourself that you are beautiful. Tell yourself that you will honor and respect yourself always. Tell yourself that you are intelligent, creative and victorious. Declare healing into your body and peace into your mind right now. Speak prosperity and abundance into your business regardless of the current circumstances. Tell yourself every day, "I will NOT be afraid," "I can conquer whatever obstacle may come my way," "I will defeat every giant thrown at me," "I can handle this life that I've been blessed with," and "I have everything that I need to accomplish what I was born to do." Doesn't that feel good to speak peace, positivity, and love over yourself?

You can either poison your spirit with your words or breathe life into your soul. Speaking life will give you the fuel to keep going when the journey of building your dreams gets tough. God said in His word, "Death and life are in the power of the tongue, and those who love it will eat its fruits" (Proverbs 18:21). This scripture is a beautiful reminder to be mindful of the words you speak and of how you use them to bring joy and encouragement to yourself and to those around you every day.

When you wake up in the morning, do you usually wake up thinking, "Oh boy, another day. I don't feel like going to work. I don't feel like making breakfast. I don't feel like ironing clothes?" Or do you wake up and try to find the joy in your today? If we are not careful, then it becomes easy to talk ourselves into a bad mood before we even get the day started.

Remember, the words you speak over your day have power. Learn to declare GOOD things over your life. Although you may not feel like making breakfast, tell yourself that you are thankful you can afford to buy groceries or use your limbs to cook. Although you may not feel like washing and folding clothes, tell yourself that you are thankful you have clothes to wear. Your mindset is important and taking control of the words you allow to spew out of your mouth will make a difference in your life.

When you feel yourself forming words to complain, to find fault, or to speak negativity, I challenge you to change your focus and to think about all the great things in your life. What is currently working out? What are you thankful for? You cannot expect to have a positive life if all you do is speak and focus on the negative things around you.

We live in a society that glorifies negativity and claps for bad behavior. You should choose to do the opposite. You can do this by not following the ways of this world, by turning away from the things that cause you to feel like you are not enough, you do not have enough, or you are not worthy of a good life.

If a certain television show or social media platform causes you to compare, condemn or criticize yourself and others, then I suggest turning away, taking a break, and finding something more productive to do with your time like reading a positive, uplifting book. The beautiful thing about life is that God granted us the freedom to choose. If you are not happy with your today, then it might be time to reevaluate the way you currently choose to speak, think and behave.

Make a list of a few things that you say out loud or ponder on throughout the day that are currently hindering your happiness. Next, write out some positive words and affirmations that can replace the negative ones. When you feel yourself speaking or thinking in a way that is not helping you, pull out your happy list and speak from that list instead. Make it a new habit to watch what you say and to do a perspective shift when your words fail to push you to thrive. Let's all choose a better, more edifying way of speaking, thinking and living!

CHAPTER 2

꧁꧂

Your Success is Your Responsibility

God has blessed us all with freedom of choice, and what you do with that freedom is completely up to you. You can choose things that are not good for you, or you can choose the opposite. It is important to think about the possible end results at the very beginning of a life choice before taking a specific path. I say this because I have bumped my head before due to not thinking and analyzing ahead of time, and it does not feel good. It actually sucks! I have since learned from my mistakes but boy did I go through a period of, "Why didn't I think first? Why the heck did I do that? I wish I could go back in time and change this or that but I can't." We all have been there and, unfortunately, making the wrong choices usually results in unanticipated consequences and overwhelming regret.

It is imperative to THINK before you act. Ask yourself several questions before you follow your emotions because you are tired of waiting, or you take an opportunity because it looks good on paper. Did you pray about it? Do you have peace about it? Where will that position or relationship lead you five years from now? What will you become on that job? Ask yourself if you are making choices that will potentially be a hindrance in the future or a positive building block. The choices you make every single day shape and create your destiny. This is why you must evaluate your choices in detail before making them.

If you are currently feeling stuck and unhappy with where you are in life, then it might be time to make some different choices. Change only comes when you make changes in your daily decisions. Make choices every day that will propel you toward the future you desire. On your journey, you will have some moments where you are not going to feel like moving forward, but you must make the choice to keep going anyway. As an entrepreneur, you might think, "What's the point of sharing my content? Why blog anymore? Why should I keep trying to build this organization when it seems like no one cares?" It is in those moments when you must dig deep within yourself to make the right decisions and to do what is right regardless of how you feel.

Choosing to stay dedicated to your dream will be so worth the temporary annoyance when your harvest starts to bloom. Those rough moments prepare you for what is to come and will build great strength inside of you. KEEP choosing to do the right thing, keep choosing to build your dreams, keep choosing to believe in yourself, and keep choosing to move forward regardless of the obstacles that will come.

Your life is like a puzzle that you are building day-by-day. You will get some pieces that just do not fit. This will come in the form of wrong relationships, dead-end jobs, making some mistakes, and being forced to choose different routes. Be sure to analyze your circumstances often and to eliminate the pieces that do not align with your goals. As soon as you discover that your relationship is not working out, your current job is not fulfilling, and that organization you joined is leading you down a path that God did not tell you to follow, make a choice to let it go.

Letting go and releasing the things that do not flow with your life's mission will be a significant part of your journey and it will assist your growth. Do not try to force anything.

Choosing to part ways with the dead things will open the door for the right opportunities to flow into your life. You will not have to force what is meant to be, so do not try to make something work if it is not falling into place naturally. Always remember you cannot go back into a time machine and change what has already been done. All you can do is learn from the past, think before you act, and start making wise choices today.

If I can be brutally honest, I do not wake up every single day singing the "happy dappy" song. Sometimes I wake up in a bad mood and do not want anything to do with this place. I, at times, will make myself go back to bed hoping to wake up in a better mood. I have learned that regardless of how I might feel, I must wake up and do what is right, treat people with kindness, and tell myself how to feel. I am human and so are you, but that is not an excuse to act poorly just because you are in a bad mood.

Your emotions will try to control you if YOU allow them to. If you do not learn to take control of your emotions, then you might make a decision you later regret. You must not compromise your future just because you did not feel great in a specific moment. Friendships end, people get into fights, they lose their jobs, and they get caught up in situations that could have been avoided only if they would have controlled their fickle emotions.

One moment you might feel full of joy, the next annoyed to the max, and then someone does something and you reach your breaking point. You have had it and you are now ready to punch the next person who looks at you in the face. What do you do in those moments? Do you just respond in a crazy manner because you "feel like it"? No, you must learn to be quiet. Tell your eyes they are not going to roll, and tell your mind to woosah, breathe, and let it go.

If you truly want to become a successful person, then you must focus on becoming successful in every area of your life. While growing a company, organization, or whatever dream you are pursuing, you will have many different emotions. Sometimes you might feel weary when people are not supporting you, a business deal does not go through, or no one registers for your event. Your mind will say, "I just don't understand." Your emotions will tell you to give up and stop trying. The question is, are you going to listen? Of course not. You must tell those little feelings to back up, and you must stay consistent and on the right path even when you do not feel motivated to do it anymore.

Success takes work and along the way, you will have a gazillion different moments of not feeling joyful. Some of your emotions will be happy and many will not be, but you cannot allow the not so great emotions to lead your day. You must decide that you are going to make it happen no matter what or how you might feel. You must push through those days when life becomes overwhelming and your emotions are screaming, "I just can't do this anymore." Yes, you can! Those voices are simply lies trying to stop you from pursuing God's purpose for your life. Your feelings will change, but your life WILL NOT if you quit now based upon your temporary emotions.

Do not allow how you feel to control what you do. You must take control of your mind. Start each day with a grateful heart, and choose to have a positive outlook on life regardless of how you currently feel. Write down five to ten positive emotions you would like to feel throughout each day, and revisit those when you are having an "annoyed with everything" moment. Re-focusing your energy on your positive list will help you maintain your composure when your emotional "I just want to scream" moments arise. Take control of those emotions now, or they will take control of you!

If you want to live a truly successful, abundant life, then you must understand that at times you might walk this journey alone. While building your dream, you might have to do it alone for months, or even a few years. Do not let that stop you. Your harvest will be worth the lonely season. You will have to give up some nights of being able to relax and instead use that time to work on your goals. It is going to take sacrifice. Even when you feel like you do not have any extra time, you will have to make time.

If you have children, a family, or a full-time job, then you might feel like it is impossible to focus on your dreams because it seems there is not enough time in each day. I challenge you to make time once the children are asleep, even if it is just twenty minutes each day. Eventually, that invested time will add up to results that would not have happened if you did not invest any time into your dream. You can still pursue your goals if you are a parent, you work full-time, or you are a full-time college student. You can still give this life your all.

I suggest creating a daily schedule and dedicating some time to your future plans. Remember, even if you can spend only ten minutes working on your vision, that is better than no minutes. I love listening to self-development messages while soaking in the bathtub, the perfect way to relax while still gaining valuable information. I also listen to audiobooks while driving instead of listening to music, the perfect way to soak up information on the go. You might need to be creative in order to do so, but I want to remind you to be intentional about making time for your future.

At times YOU will be the only person who believes in your dream and that can see the bigger picture. Some people might even tell you that you have completely lost your mind, you are weird, or your dream cannot come true. Some will think you are dreaming too big and will try to discourage you along the way. You know those people that say, "But wait, you're dead broke. How in the world do you expect to finance that big grand dream you have in your head?" Or, "You can't build a business from the ground up; you will fail because most businesses fail within the first few years, and you have no business experience." Not to mention, "How do you expect to start that organization and teach others when you didn't graduate high school?" You must tune out those negative voices immediately. You must block out all outside noise that does not line up with where God is leading you.

Do not allow someone who cannot understand your God-given vision to talk you out of going after your destiny. You might not know how but if you are obedient to the

Lord, then He will show you how little by little. You must surround yourself with like-minded individuals because they will understand the path better than someone who decided to go with the flow and follow the norm. My advice to you is, if you want to live a purpose-filled abundant life, then do not follow the crowd. I suggest doing the complete opposite of what you see the masses doing. RUN the other way. God tells us in His word, "Do not conform to this world but be ye transformed by the renewal of your mind" (Romans 12:2). I take that scripture literally. Do not allow the normal way of thinking and living life to control you.

Think outside the box and allow your creative juices to flow. It is also important to pray and to keep some dreams to yourself. You do not need to shout your plans from the mountain tops. If you focus on doing the work, then eventually your results will speak for you. You will even have to cast down your own negative thoughts and the little voices inside your head that tell you how it is not going to work out. Do not listen to those voices! Use your mouth to speak life over your dreams and continue to tell yourself that you can do it regardless of what your life currently looks like.

While building your empire, prepare to be your own cheerleader, encourager, and marketing king or queen. You will have to market yourself, especially in the beginning of launching your brand, business or organization. Yes, people might get tired of you persistently marketing your services, your book, your organization, your products or your live broadcast. They might even unfollow, unfriend or block you, and that is okay. They were not your true supporters anyway.

You cannot concern yourself with the people who do not support you. It would not matter if you only shared your business once a year, some people would not like you, support you, or cheer for you simply because you are you. Some of those non-supporters might even be envious that you are willing to take a risk and you are being rewarded because of it. You also must remember that some people will not root for you to win because they are not even rooting for themselves to win.

Some people will hate the progress you are making and will not support you because they are afraid to step out and try something new themselves. Do not invest any ounce of your energy into those that are not rooting for your destiny. How people might feel about you is none of your concern. If you know that you are trying your best to do good in this world, and you are making a positive impact that will change lives, then that is what you must place your focus on. Do not focus on trying to win everyone's approval.

I fully understand that in order to have a successful company, you will need people to support your business or to buy your book, product or service, but you must have the right people in mind. Your task is to figure out your target market and to market your services to them. Ask yourself: "Who is my target market? How old are they? What's their income? What's their age range? What problem am I solving for them? What's their greatest concern? How can my service add value to their lives?" The more details you gather about your target audience the more equipped you will be to build your brand. You also will not feel as much stress once you identify your target market and promote your brand to the individuals that need your services because you will not be trying to appeal to everyone.

Sharing your organization, company and brand with the right people is crucial. Of course, if you sell tires, then someone in search of shoes probably will not be interested in your service. Your job is to find people in need of the service you offer, and those are the people with whom you want to share your information. Once you identify the people that need your service, consistently add value to their lives. They will eventually support you.

Remember that you are building trust and forming relationships day-by-day. Do not take the people that support and love what you do for granted, and do not focus on the ones that do not, even if they are family members or high school friends. You cannot place your attention on them. Instead, develop an "I don't care what people think about me" attitude and release yourself from mental bondage, especially when you know that you are doing everything with a genuine heart. You must learn to be free from the fear of other people's opinion of you.

Regardless of what you do, some people will have something to say, good or bad, so why invest any energy into their opinions? If you have been fearful in this area, then right now is the time to release those fears for good. Make a commitment to yourself that you will not invest any more of your precious time trying to be a people pleaser. You must continue to move forward and to be an inspiration despite the validation of others. God will bring the right people into your life and open the right doors at the right time if you simply stay obedient in the midst of feeling like you are going at it alone. Please know that your journey is inspiring so many people even if they never tell you. By simply taking a leap of faith, your life story will be a blessing to others.

I speak from personal experience with growing my health company Be A Health Nut Too. I thought people would be happy for me, root for me, and cheer for me. You would think that people would cheer for those that are trying to make a positive change and impact around the world. You would think that people would be excited to see anyone trying to spread inspiration around the world. Boy was I wrong! Even some people that I grew up with, high school friends, pageant friends, associates, and some family members, did not encourage me along the way.

Honestly, at first, it made me a bit sad to think about the response of non-supportive people, especially those that were supposed to be close to me. I quickly had to learn to get over that sadness and realize that when God places purpose on the inside of you, He will lead and guide you along the way. I learned not to place my hope in people or to expect them to be happy for the doors that God was opening in my life.

I learned that it was not about receiving praise from people. People often support you one day then bash you the next. I learned to do what I was doing from a place of love, obedience, and passion. I learned how to surrender my own plans to God's plans for my life, even when I was uncomfortable or became discouraged when people were not supportive. I stopped focusing on who did or did not cheer for me. I truly stopped caring. If they supported the brand, cool; if not, I continued moving forward anyway.

I just want to be a blessing to everyone I meet, to be obedient to the Lord, and to inspire as many people as I can while living on this earth. I want to leave a legacy of spreading positivity, sowing good seeds, and living my life as a vessel of God's love. My purpose stands on much more than some applause, likes on social media, or people saying "congrats". I am not going to pretend that it does not feel good when someone compliments you or tells you how much of an inspiration you have been in their lives. Everyone on this earth enjoys being loved, complimented and appreciated. However, I do not place my focus on receiving approval from humans anymore.

My deepest desire is for God to be pleased with my life, with the seeds that I have sown, with the harvest that my life has produced, and with the lives that I have touched in a positive way. I want God to say to me on the day of judgement, "well done my good and faithful servant." That is the greatest reward any of us can receive. So no matter how many people may want to see you fail or how much applause you receive, keep going and give it absolutely no attention. Keep your focus on producing quality content and on building your brand every single day. Keep your focus on following the purpose that you believe God gave you.

One day you will look up and all that hard work will pay off so big, and some of those same people that were not cheering for you, in the beginning, will ask you to teach them how you achieved those results. Continue to believe in yourself, to market yourself, to encourage yourself, and to keep planting those seeds NON-STOP! Your sweet harvest is near!

CHAPTER 3

༄

Let Go of What's Hindering You

Keep the door to your past slammed shut. Do not revisit what you perceive as failures. I know this is easier said than done, and I have had to learn to stop running back to my past disappointments as well. I used to love competing in pageants and when I did not win, I viewed it as a failure. I would be so upset. I prepared for months, spent SO much money, but did not win the crown. However, I had to change my perspective and view my pageant years as a season of major growth. I met so many lifelong friends, learned how to present myself in a professional manner, and learned how to speak confidently in front of thousands of people. Competing in pageants birthed a confidence inside of me that I never knew existed.

Those years of competing prepared me for what I am doing today. I am no longer afraid to give a live presentation. I now can walk into an interview with confidence, and I know how to truly believe in myself. I learned that even if I did not walk away with a crown on my head each time, I walked away with more knowledge, confidence, and inspiration. That season prepared me to be a faith walker; it taught me to be willing to invest thousands of dollars into my dreams, to punch my own fears in the face, and to take a risk even if it did not turn out how I expected. I learned to let go of reminding myself of the times that I did not succeed and I tried again.

I would pay another entry fee and compete over and over again. I eventually did win a few pageant titles because I remained consistent, learned from each experience, and refused to let my past disappointments discourage me. It was important to change my focus, to let go, and to stop reminding myself of all the times I did not take the title, crown and sash home. I had to remind myself that I won in a different way.

If your past frustrations keep resurfacing in your mind, or if you find yourself often reflecting on all the things that did not work out, then I want to encourage you to pay attention to everything that you have gained and learned from your past thus far. It is often scary to step out on faith if you have tried something before and it did not go as planned (I know this feeling all too well). Therefore, it is important to shift your perspective and to view your "failures" as educational periods in your life.

You can learn so much from every attempt to try something new. Every successful person that you see today, failed their way to success. No one has had the perfect journey. Everyone experiences stumbling blocks along the way. Success might look easy, but I assure you that it is not. Do not be afraid to try, try, and try again until you figure out what works; this will lead you to success.

You might be thinking that you have made too many terrible mistakes, or that you are stuck and there is no way out of the mess that you are in. I am here to tell you that you can change your life with one decision: simply try. You are not your past or your mistakes. You are human, you can learn from your mistakes, and you can use them to build an amazing future.

Use your past to fuel you. Use your mistakes to propel you to success. The time is now to make a change in your own life, and in the lives of others. Let go of the "I can't do it" mentality. What you believe about yourself is true for you; therefore, you must believe the best in the midst of your past disappointments. God is all-powerful and has the ability to do what seems impossible to our human minds. Even the things that have led to major consequences can be used for good.

In Romans 8:28, God tells us, "We know that all things work together for good to those who love God, to those who are called according to His purpose." This scripture is an amazing reminder that even our past mishaps can be used for good and for God's glory. Your testimony can be the reminder that someone else needs to keep going and to let go of what hinders them. Your ability to let go and to keep your focus on the things that uplift you can help someone else turn their life around. Meditate on this scripture often and allow it to be a gentle reminder that great things are headed your way.

You might believe that there is no way you can be successful because your family members lived in poverty and that all you have ever been exposed to was "the struggle". I totally understand and have been right where you are. I did not have any examples of a super successful person growing up. I did not have any family members that owned their own businesses. I grew up in a poverty-stricken area and could have easily taken the easy road, instead of the path less traveled. I decided that I wanted nothing to do with a struggled-filled life and that I had to be willing to fight for the life I desired. I wanted more for myself, my future husband and my future children.

I could have drifted down a negative, broken path because of my childhood. I grew up fatherless and that experience could have led me down a path of making negative choices. However, I decided to use EVERY hard, rough and unfair experience to make me a better person. I did not allow my past to cripple me. I used those experiences to push me and inspire me to create a different life than what I had experienced growing up, and you can do the same.

I learned so much from my father while he was in prison. He taught me to get my education, to stay focused on my career, and to always consider the potential consequences of my future decisions. I learned that one mistake could alter my destiny, so I have always tried to make the right choices. I have not been perfect in any way, shape or form, but I have learned from my mistakes and have continued moving forward. I am thankful that my father helped me gain valuable insight during his prison sentence. His experience taught me to stay on the right path in spite of not always having an ideal childhood.

I want to challenge you to not compare your future to what you have experienced in the past. You must look beyond what your eyes can currently see. Decide today that you will not be bound to "poverty thinking" but you will believe in the abundance of all the good around you. God is the supplier of your every need and can take care of you.

Starting now, let go of every thought that limits you. Your thinking blocks your blessings and stops you from moving forward. Decide today that you will trust that good things can and will happen to you. Every thought you have that attempts to turn you away from pursuing your goals is a fear-based thought. Therefore, you must fight back, believe the best, and take control of your mind. Let go of everything that hinders you from living the life you desire. Rid your life of every person speaking defeat over you, or every circumstance that keeps you stuck, and choose to seek a new way of life. God gave us the beautiful freedom to decide which path to take in life, and it is totally up to you.

No other person will save you; you must do it for yourself. I know that this is easier said than done, but you must be willing to put in the mental and physical work required to change your life. It might require you to reach out and seek guidance from someone who has already succeeded in the area you are seeking to grow in or learn about. Having people around you that have expertise in a specific area can be extremely beneficial. You will be able to gain valuable wisdom from them that can help propel you forward and keep you from making certain errors along the way. Do not be afraid to ask questions and ask for help when you need it.

Pray and ask God to show you how to release what no longer serves you, and to reveal the direction He wants you to follow. Creating your own future or being your own boss takes WORK, passion, persistence, and true dedication. If it were easy, then everyone would do it. Your dream will take some sleepless nights, your dream will take letting go of some toxic relationships, and your dream will take you choosing to invest in yourself even when you do not "feel" like it. The sweet news is when you decide to do the work, and start to see results, your victory will be worth every trial, every disappointment, and everything you sacrificed along the way. When your harvest finally comes from all the sacrifices you will make, you will be so happy that you learned to let go of everything that was stopping you!

Overall, your environment matters. If you are constantly hanging around people that are speaking defeat into your ears and telling you why you cannot do this or that, then it is time to make some relationship adjustments in your life. Why? You become like those you are around the most. If you are always around pessimistic or negative people that complain, gossip and entertain drama, then some of their habits will eventually rub off on you. Evaluate your circle of friends and distance yourself from anyone who is potentially leading you down the wrong path. Do not feel bad for upgrading your surroundings; your future life depends on it!

Ask yourself how you feel when you are around certain people. Do you feel encouraged, uplifted, positive, loved, respected, ambitious and righteous? Or do you feel discouraged, depressed, negative, rejected, downcast and sorrowful? Your friends should speak life over you, pray for you, encourage you, believe in you and tell you the truth, and you should be able to do the same for them. Are your friends asking you to read a positive inspirational book, to attend a business seminar, to participate in a life coaching class, to create a positive organization, or to attend church? Or are they constantly asking you to get drunk, party, smoke, steal, and pressure you to do things that you know will lead you down a path full of regret? I am sure you catch my drift.

You must surround yourself with people that will hold you accountable and tell you if you are not making the best decisions. You might say, "But wait, I hang out with my family, my boyfriend, or my best friend and they are pressuring me to go down the wrong path. I can't just cut my loved ones off. I'd feel bad and I don't want to be mean." My answer to that is simple: you have to love some people from a distance. You might need to break off a bad relationship that is not going anywhere anyway. If that man or woman is influencing you to do things that you know you should not be doing, then is that really the person you want to spend the rest of your life with? It is time to raise your standards and to stand up for what you deserve. You do not have to settle for anything less than God's absolute best for your life.

There is nothing wrong with being honest! Tell your family member or your significant other that you are going to take some time away to focus on yourself. Explain that you have some areas in your personal life that you must work on to become the best version of yourself. Tell them you are making some changes in your life and you cannot hang out like you used to anymore. Be honest and tell them that the environments you are in and the choices you are making are negatively impacting your life. Tell them you love them but must do what is best for you at this time and you want to do things a bit different.

It is not that you can never hang out with your family anymore, but maybe you can invite them over for dinner at your house where you control the environment. Now if it is a bad relationship that you are choosing to let go of, then I suggest breaking it off completely, never looking back, and trusting God to bring the right person into your life at the right time. At the end of the day, YOU are the main person who has to live with the consequences or rewards from the decisions you make.

Your future is counting on you. God says in His word that "bad company corrupts good character" (1 Corinthians 15:33), so you cannot hang out with just any and everyone. You want to be set apart. It is not mean that you are making a positive decision for your future. You are choosing to live a better life. When you seek greatness, you just cannot do what most people do.

Raising your standards will come with losing some people along the way. People might even judge you or talk about you, but do not worry; that is not your concern. If your family and friends truly love you, then they will understand and be supportive of your decision to work on creating a better life for yourself. If you find it difficult to release the destructive things in your life, then remind yourself that you cannot live a positive life while hanging around negative influences.

You must be the example. When you decide to change your life, it affects not only your life but also the lives of others. People will begin to tell you how much you have changed. Take that as a compliment; it means that you are not the old you, you have grown, and you have become a better person. Decide to become the leader of your own life, regardless of whether everyone agrees with your decision or not. You do not want to wake up one day with a life full of regrets all because you wanted to be a people-pleaser, you did not want to say "no", and you followed the crowd. Other people do not have to live with your consequences, or possible regret, so you must do what is best for you.

If you do not have many people that you can surround yourself with that are going in the same direction that you want to follow, then my advice is to seek a mentor, find a local success group, or read books from those that have succeeded in the area in which you are looking to succeed. It is important to learn from other successful people. Books, inspirational CDs and motivational speakers on YouTube have been major blessings for me on my faith journey. Instead of spending hours a day on social media, I take time to read, to study, to write out my goals, and to discover ways to work toward them. For those of you who may not know what you feel led to do just yet, that is totally okay. It may take some time to discover your purpose. I discovered a part of my purpose by experiencing health issues and deciding to take better care of my health. I had no idea it would eventually turn into a health company and a means to help others.

If you are still trying to discover your path, then I suggest surrounding yourself with people that are go-getters and learn from them. Let their drive motivate you. Let their success encourage you so that you can be successful, too. Ask them how they did it, what books they read, who mentored them, and what advice they could give to you. Your inner circle and who you interact with on a daily basis are crucial for your success. Their mindset for greatness will start to rub off on you and motivate you to get started on your journey. I suggest doing what you need to do to set yourself apart and to grow in your own lane. Even if that means cramming your head into books daily, listening to motivational speakers, and attending weekly success meet-ups, then it will truly change and alter the direction of your life.

CHAPTER 4

❧

Discover Your Purpose and Path

I must say that it is quite a process figuring out what you were created to do, right? At times life can feel like an up and down roller coaster while trying to figure everything out. It can be SO overwhelming and just plain confusing! None of us were born with a "how to live the perfect life" step-by-step guide. Many of us have been figuring out this thing called life day-by-day. Discovering your purpose is not as simple as doing what you love. I know many people have preached that whatever you love to do is the calling for your life. However, I do not fully agree with this statement because some of the things that we as humans "love" doing might not be leading us down a promising path.

Some people love smoking, so should they teach other people the perfect way to puff a cigarette or marijuana to make themselves feel better or to escape pain? Some people love to stay in relationships that harm them physically and emotionally, so should they go and teach others to do the same? Of course not! So you might be asking, well then how in the world do I discover my purpose?

I can speak only from personal experience with the whole purpose thing. I had no intentions of starting a health company or writing this book. I actually experienced some VERY frustrating health issues in the past. I could not digest food properly, I had severe acne flare-ups, I was anemic, and I experienced hormonal imbalances. While my health seemed to be declining, it led me to look into taking better care of my body by way of proper nutrition.

I moved to Los Angeles with my mind on what I believed was my "purpose" following the "do what you love" philosophy. I wanted to be on television. I graduated college with a degree in communications and I moved out to the west coast to pursue what I thought I loved doing. After only a few months of living in Los Angeles, I was already enrolled in television hosting classes, sharpening my skills, and getting my audition reel together, then all of a sudden I felt led to start a health blog. Wait, what? I immediately said, "No, I'm not starting a health anything. I barely know how to cook, I'm still learning the basics, I'm not interested in that direction, it's not my purpose, and I want to be on TV."

I made SO many excuses and for a few months, I disobeyed God's instructions. I wanted to follow the plans I had for my life since high school, not start some new journey that I was still discovering for myself. I never knew God would use my life, my health issues, and my frustrations to build a health and wellness company. I never thought I would teach and encourage others to nourish their temples and to fight off diseases simply by using nature. I never knew I would be able to offer healthy alternative products that are chemical free and do not harm the body. I had no idea what God was doing through me when I first started the Be A Health Nut Too health blogging journey.

I was SO frustrated that I had to experience health issues; I did not understand "why me". I cried sometimes because of it. I just wanted to be normal and not have to deal with my body not functioning properly. Now I actually see the reason I needed to learn about healing my body from the inside out, treating my body like God's holy temple, the importance of eating healthy foods, and not taking my health for granted. I am able to use everything that I learned to be a blessing to others. Through my pain, I truly discovered one of my assignments on this earth. I turned something negative into something positive and I now use it to enlighten others. How amazing is that?

The very thing that made me "not normal" in my eyes turned out to be a way to assist other people in their healing. Sometimes the main thing that you wish would go away could be the answer you are seeking to discover your purpose on this earth. Your pain might be the testimony that someone else needs to keep going and not give up. Your hardships might be birthing your purpose. How can you turn a negative situation in your life into something positive? How can you help others? If you are currently battling with a situation that seems impossible, then I pray for restoration, understanding, and healing over you. I pray that you are able to come out on the other side of whatever you might be facing and that your story will be a blessing to so many. I pray that your purpose is revealed in the midst of your pain and that you are able to use it for the glory of our Lord.

I learned it was all about me changing my perspective. I needed to endure a few health battles in order to be able to gain an understanding of natural healing. It allows me to now speak from a level of experience and faith that I would not have known if I always had perfect health. I am thankful that I was obedient and followed what I felt led to do regardless of how I initially felt about it. God has a beautiful way of working everything out for your good, even the bad stuff.

So I believe your purpose is not always all about you. It is not always about what makes you feel good. It is not always about what you love or want to do. Now I do believe God knows the desires of our hearts and at times He will bless you to absolutely love what you do. I have SO much passion and love for living a healthy lifestyle, and for helping others with their journey now, BUT I was not born that way. I had my own plans, but decided to lay them down to follow God's path instead of my own and birthed one of my purposes in the process. God may be leading you to India to help build homes, to care for abandoned children, to pray for the sick, to create an organization for the homeless, or simply to be a good wife and mother. You may not initially care to do what you feel led to do, but I believe your purpose will bless others, be a way to share God's love, and eventually bless you, too.

I encourage you to pray and ask God for a clear sign and for peace about what you should be doing with your life. I often pray "not my will but yours be done" and I follow my peace and trust the Lord with my journey every day. Keep your eyes off of the path that others travel. Do not try to copy anyone else because God has a specific purpose created just for you. I believe we all should pray for guidance and be led by God in the choices that we make, instead of by our own selfish desires. What gifts has the Lord naturally blessed you with? What can you naturally do well without even thinking about it? Can you sing really well? Do you encourage others? Do you love giving back?

Exploring your natural and spiritual gifts could lead you to your answer. If you have a gift of praying over other people, then your calling could be starting a prayer ministry at your local church home. If you have the gift of encouraging, then your purpose could be uplifting those around you as an inspirational speaker. If you have the gift of giving, then your gift could be starting a local pantry for the homeless or volunteering at a senior living house. If you have the gift of serving others, then your calling could be assisting local teachers with after school youth programs. We all have our own special path and gifts from the Lord.

You have to simply step out on faith to discover if you are on the right track.

Have you experienced a hardship that God delivered you from? You could use that testimony to bless others. Maybe you should write a book or start a weekly encouragement podcast. Personally, I believe our true purpose on earth is not about us. It is about bringing glory to the Lord, serving others, spreading love, and being used as a vessel in whatever way God sees fit. Ask yourself if what you are doing brings pleasure and joy to you only, or if it inspires, encourages, helps or serves those around you. No one can tell you your exact purpose but the One who created you! Seek God, pray for answers, follow your peace, evaluate your natural gifts, and know that your greatest pain or lesson could be birthing your greatest life purpose.

You also might find some inspiration and insight from the successful people around you. This is completely okay; we all have role models that we admire and follow people that are living the life we would like to experience for ourselves. There is absolutely nothing wrong with being inspired by someone who has done the work, who has continued moving forward during the hard seasons, and who is now living an abundant purpose-filled life. Just do not allow comparison to creep into your heart and rob you of your own journey. Instead of you finding your own way, you will begin to duplicate what someone else is doing then get mad if you do not produce the same exact results. If you find yourself starting to obsess over someone else's blessings so much that you are losing sight of the path God is leading you to, then you might need to step back, focus your attention on solutions to help you grow, and take your eyes off of everyone else.

Choose to admire people from a distance and to not make another human or their blessings your idol. Do not covet what someone else has or try to follow their A-B-C step-by-step guidelines. You have NO idea what that person had to endure to have what they have, or what they are currently facing or battling to keep it. If you ever find yourself thinking *I wish I had that person's life*, then remind yourself that you only see what is shown to you on a social media feed. You are not truly seeing the behind-the-scenes battles, struggles or victories that person experiences daily.

Furthermore, remember to keep a positive perspective and to not allow yourself to become so consumed with what someone else has going on. It will only distract you from focusing on making your own dreams come true. God put you on this earth for a specific purpose that only YOU can fulfill. Put your energy into discovering who you really are, walk your own journey, carve your own path, and lead the way for others to be inspired by what God does through you. Your life and story truly matter. Your victories, your bumps in the road, your past lessons, and the wisdom you have gained along the way can be used to uplift those around you. You were not put on this earth to be anyone other than yourself.

It is perfectly fine to study books, listen to inspirational messages, and gain wisdom on how to do something new. It is totally okay to study what you should do to become a better person from those that are living the life you desire to live. Just do not place other people on a pedestal or try to replicate every little thing that they do. Your energy should be focused on making your vision come to fruition, and not on trying to be the next whoever it is that you admire most. You must take gems of wisdom from each of those individuals then use that information to become a version of yourself that you never knew existed. Be grateful for every gift that you have been blessed with, work on personal growth every day, pray and ask for wisdom, then decide DAILY to work on becoming the person, the friend, the teacher, the artist, the author, the business owner, the wife, the husband, and the blessing you were created to be!

This society has conditioned people to constantly compete against one another, to compare your life to the next person's life, and to replicate what seems popular. God created you with a specific life mission, with beautiful UNIQUE gifts, and you should not have your eyes on anyone else's life. If you find yourself always looking at what other people are doing, and it causes you to put unnecessary pressure on yourself to accomplish "this or that", then it is time to pull away from everything that distracts you.

You are enough and you should not allow yourself to feel inferior just because your life does not look like your next-door neighbor's life. Mental programming runs rampant in this day and age. It causes people to place their focus on everything else besides becoming the very best version of themselves. The only person that you should try to outdo is the person you were in the past. Each day you should push yourself to be better than you were the day before. We live in a world of abundance and what is for you my dear, is for you. Before you were born, the script of your life was already written. Your destiny awaited you even then. Therefore, it is up to you to make the right decisions and to go after your God-given destiny.

If you are allowing any outside influences to stop you from pursuing your purpose, then you are hindering yourself and must break free right now. You must free your mind from any strongholds, or from any self-sabotaging mental bondage that holds you back. You must cast down the lies in your head telling you that you are not enough, you are not talented, and you do not have the means to pursue the life you desire.

Be free from scarcity thinking and know that what you need will come to you at the perfect time. You might say, "Yes, I hear you, but I can't even pay my bills right now." Do not focus on poverty or the feeling of lack. Poverty consciousness, or poverty thinking, can be detrimental to your future. It causes you to constantly focus on shortage, or not having enough. Also, poverty thinking can cause envy and bitterness to grow inside of your heart and put pressure on you to keep up with everyone else. If you frown upon other people's success, and you find yourself getting upset because it seems like everyone else is being blessed, then you might be dealing with poverty consciousness.

Here are a few questions that may help you understand your thinking better: Do you find yourself constantly feeling like there is not enough financial abundance to go around? Do you purposely withhold valuable information from other people that you know could help them succeed because you are afraid they might climb the corporate ladder before you do? Do you find yourself looking down on people that have made it to a level of affluence that you would like to reach? Or do you ever say to yourself that some people are just lucky and you feel success could never happen for you? Were you raised in a household where your parents always said "money doesn't grow on trees" and because of that you now have a negative outlook on financial freedom? If you answered yes to any of the above questions, then it is important to be mindful of how that kind of thinking can hold you back from reaching your true potential. Poor thinking does not produce favorable results but is harmful to your mental health. I want you to know that if you are willing to put in the work, then your victory will eventually come and before you know it, you will be scratching goal after goal off your list of accomplishments.

How do I know these things? I am speaking from personal experience. I know firsthand what it is like to grow up in a community where hardships and shortages persist. I grew up in what many refer to as the "hood", where drug dealers were on the street corners at night, and many people lived in poverty. I decided at an early age that I wanted nothing to do with living a lifestyle of constant struggle. It was a personal choice and I decided not to settle for the life that I saw around me. I wanted more and I was willing to grind for it.

You must trust that God, who created you, will provide your every need. I want to challenge you to listen to yourself. Do not dwell on what you do not have; do not think about why you cannot accomplish this or that because YOU are listening to you. GET OUT OF YOUR OWN WAY! Free your mind from the mental torment of feeling like you will never have enough, or be enough, or that you will never make it. You can prosper and have a good life. Everything will work out for you if you simply believe and do the work. It is time to build your faith muscle. It does not matter what everything around you looks like; our Lord can change your circumstances in the blink of an eye. Decide today that you will use your faith to focus on the good you desire, and on using the gifts that God has placed on the inside of you.

God has always made a way for me, even when I had no idea of what to do next, where to go, or how to start. I prayed and I simply followed my heart and peace. I encouraged myself and put my faith to work and you must do the same. I moved from Flint, Michigan to Las Vegas, Nevada and then from Vegas to Los Angeles, California. I had no job, barely had a savings, had no idea where I would live, and did not know anyone but I took the leap of faith anyway. Was I scared? Heck YES! I was leaving everything I ever knew, my family, friends, and even some relationships that I held near and dear to my heart. It even saddened me at times that I had to move away and leave my comfort zone behind; however, I was not going to let my feelings stop me from following my dreams.

I knew that I was my only competition, and getting to where I desired to be was just a matter of me being obedient, believing, and following the call that God had on my life. I trusted that God would continue to provide for me just as He did in the past. Now looking back years later, I am so grateful that I decided to believe in myself and jump. I challenged myself and I focused on my own journey. I never knew I would write a book (I am not the writing type), but here I am writing a book to encourage each of you to do the same. Do not let fear control you. I live each day by faith, even when I feel afraid. I am telling you what I know from personal experience and now it is time for you to activate your faith muscle and to speak those things that are not as though they are. Learn to declare victory over your dreams. Learn to believe beyond what your eyes can see. Wake up every day determined to become a stronger, more resilient, more beautiful version of yourself.

If you do not know how to do something, then study from someone who does. This does not mean copy what they do, but you can take notes from them. So let's say someone has a successful fashion blog and you would like to launch your own. I suggest that you visit their blog and look at how many times they post a week, what fashion topics they discuss, what posts receive the most engagements, and what catches your eye the most. Then you can model your blog in a similar fashion. This does not mean use the exact same blog title, theme or description, but you can use their blog as a reference for what works and what does not work.

You will still want to create your own unique style of blogging and to make sure that you are not the exact same as everyone else. This will help your website stand out and give your readers something to look forward to that has its own distinctive vibe. So if the blogger you admire shared a post with the title "How to Rock a Maxi Dress Ten Different Ways" and that blog had a substantial amount of engagement from his or her subscribers, then that information lets you know that people are interested in maxi dresses. You could then make a blog about how to rock cute maxi dresses and make them a statement piece on any vacation. In essence, you are sharing the same topic but in a different way.

When you are inspired by someone in the same field, it is okay to learn from them and to apply the information you learn to your own journey. You do not need to compete with them or compare your journey to theirs; simply apply the knowledge to keep growing along your own path. Allow other people to motivate you if you feel yourself starting to compare, and let it be a reminder that if they can make it, then you can, too!

Look at yourself in the mirror right now and say, "I can do whatever I put my mind to", "I will not fear", "I am strong", "I am well-equipped and able", "I have no lack", "I am abundant", "I am beautiful", "I have great favor wherever I go", and "I will live a life of purpose and change the lives of those around me in a positive way!" How did that make you feel? It feels good to speak positivity and life over your circumstances. Shift your energy from all negative self-defeating thoughts that make you feel bad and instead look for ways to build yourself up every day.

You are the person that you must outdo. You are the person who has to live with the life you have created, no one else! You are the person who gets to celebrate the accomplishments that come from the hard work you invest. You are the person who also has to deal with the regret of allowing fear to cripple you. Fear will tell you to never take a BIG chance; do not listen to that voice. Dig deep within yourself and make a decision that will move you closer to the life you desire each and every day. You can be your biggest cheerleader or your worst enemy. Choose to love yourself, to embrace your gifts, to never compare, and to accomplish those dreams stored deep inside of you! Allow your gifts to flourish! Fight for your future! You can do this! I believe in you but the question is, do YOU believe in you?

CHAPTER 5

❦

Endure Through Hard Seasons

We have all experienced times in our lives where things were not working out and it is simply frustrating. You know that place where you give something your absolute all but you do not get the results you expected or wanted? Instead of pushing through, you decide it would be easier to give up. You might say, "I'm just going to do away with this project", "I am over putting in all this darn work for nothing", or "it's pointless and I'm not getting any results." You think to yourself, *Why put all of my energy into something that isn't yielding a harvest? I am wasting time and should just quit.* I have been there SO many times. I have wanted to scream. I have cried. I have vented to my closest friends. I have prayed. I have worried. I have wanted to give up and crawl into a little hole. I have felt purposeless and like no one cared. I know firsthand what it feels like to not want to try anymore. I have been in that dark mental space, but I realized that none of that harmful thinking helped. It actually made things worse.

The negative, "woe is me" mindset blocked my ability to create. I had to conquer my poor attitude; I had to take control of my emotions and make a decision. I could not allow my emotions to lead me any longer because they caused me to drift into a depression. When you are feeling low and empty, you must find the strength to keep your head up. I found inner strength by discovering my *why*. I could not just give up because I knew my dream was so much bigger than me. I knew God was going to use my vision to help encourage other people. If I would have given up, then I would not have been able to share my testimony and help other people overcome their struggles and hardships. I wanted to be a role model for my family and for future generations. I knew that if I hung in there, things would get better and I would be able to be a living testament of not throwing in the towel when the journey becomes challenging.

During my rough moments, I grew stronger, God developed me, and I learned valuable lessons. I continuously reminded myself that one day it would all be worth the temporary discomfort. One day I would be able to help someone else birth their dream, and encourage many people to keep going even if everything around them tells them to stop. I woke up every day, despite how I felt, and reminded myself that this journey was bigger than my emotions, that I needed to push past the uncomfortable moments and keep moving forward. In my darkest times, I was left with two decisions: I could take the easy route and stop working toward my dreams because life was hard and no one was supporting my vision, or I could keep moving forward despite how I felt. Regardless of what my situation looked like, I decided to keep going, which is why you are reading this book today.

I realized that it is not always going to be easy; the road to success simply takes work and TIME. I remember a time when I wanted to partner with a larger company to help me with branding and they told me "no" because I was just starting out and was not big enough. I cried. I am not going to lie, it hurt my feelings because I worked my tail off and would not have taken that opportunity for granted. I believed that everyone starts somewhere, and that it was simply rude to just write someone off because they are not "big" enough. What the heck? I decided to let it go and keep trusting God to expand my territory in His perfect timing and not try to force my brand to expand on my own.

I learned that in order to truly live the life you desire, you must be willing to hear "no". You must be willing to have doors closed in your face. You MUST become your biggest fan, and you must keep going when other people are not cheering for you. You cannot care about who is or who is not rooting for you. Take your eyes off of how difficult the process may seem and shift your focus to solutions. Instead of wallowing in sorrow because an opportunity did not work out, take some time to write down your goals in as much detail as possible, create plans for how to execute them, and then go out and make it happen.

Let's say you would like to launch a podcast on "empowerment". First, consider the following questions: Why do you want to do a podcast? What sets you apart? What makes you unique? Who's your target audience? Then write out a deadline for the date that you would like to launch. Next, write out the topics you would like to discuss. What broadcast network do you feel would work best for your podcast (YouTube, Periscope, IGTV, etc.)? Do you plan to bring guest speakers on your show? If so, who would you like to bring on the podcast and why would they be a valuable guest speaker? How will you entice them to come on your podcast? Where would you like to see your podcast six months after its launch? How do you plan to market it and expand your reach?

I suggest creating deadlines for the miniature goals that will help you achieve your major goals. Do not panic if you go a bit over your anticipated date. You still have a concrete goal to work toward. It is important to be detailed with what, why and how you plan to make your vision come to life. Get very clear about what you are planning to do, set a daily or monthly to-do list, check off tasks as you complete them, and know your *why*. This will keep you on track when the journey gets rocky and things do not run smoothly. Yes, the journey is tough, but so are you. You can do this. You must decide to have a NO MATTER WHAT attitude about your life. Dig in deep and tell yourself every day, "I will make a way" and "I will not give up on my purpose just because the road is hard right now."

If you are not receiving the results you desire, then it might be time to adjust your plans, change your approach, and try different strategies until you find what works. You must also understand the planting process. If you plant carrot seeds on Monday, then carrots will not blossom on Tuesday. You must continue to water those seeds, allow them to get sunlight, and pluck the weeds. In due time, the carrots will sprout. When you experience a rough moment, you must remind yourself that it is the same planting process when it comes to your dreams; they will not bloom overnight. Continue to sow those seeds, water them, and pluck those negative mental weeds (thoughts), and eventually your harvest will yield beautiful results.

Things can work out for you, but you must keep moving forward. I am a living testimony to this statement. I continued on when no one knew about my health company. I continued promoting when I did not have that many people cheering for me. I continued moving forward before I had positive customer reviews because I was determined to follow the vision God placed on my heart. I had to keep trusting His plans, put one foot in front of the other, and keep doing the work required to finally see some results. When I look back on how far I have come, it amazes me that Be A Health Nut Too products are now inside a few stores. How crazy is that? And to think, I almost threw it all away just because the journey was hard, the birthing process did not feel good, and I was not yet seeing any results.

Overtime, my consistency started paying off. I am thankful I did not listen to my crazy, emotional roller coaster moments where I wanted to quit; instead I kept going. You can do this just like I did and any other successful person you see. It is going to take time, you are going to experience many moments of "I just can't do this anymore, and you are going to want to stop. However, you cannot stop. During those moments you must have self-encouragement sessions and tell yourself that your results will be worth the temporary pain. When you start to feel a bit overwhelmed, take time to pull away from everything, pray, release those worries, and do something that you really enjoy.

If you are feeling empty, stressed and depressed, then you will not be able to create or to pour into others. It is important to make sure that you are being filled with positive messages and surrounding yourself with positive people daily. Make it a habit to read and listen to inspirational music and messages for at least forty-five minutes a day. This will encourage you, inspire you, fill you, and push you to keep going in the midst of any storm.

If you give up now, then you will never know what you could have accomplished, you will have to keep starting over, and you will grow old with regret. Keep going regardless of how you currently feel. Greatness truly takes time, patience, consistency, persistence, and a belief in yourself. In due time, if you keep building brick by brick every single day, then your hard work will pay off! One great example of a person who stayed persistent when life kept knocking him down is the motivational speaker Leslie Calvin "Les" Brown. His story and journey to success is one of my absolute favorites. He was labeled "educable mentally retarded", was born in an abandoned apartment building, was adopted, grew up in poverty, and fought to become one of the greatest and highest paid public speakers in the world. He was told "no" time and time again but did not let that stop him. He was persistent, determined, and hungry for success. Two of his favorite phrases that inspire me are "You have greatness inside you" and "It is possible". I just love those statements because they are so true, and his life is a living testament to both.

Do not expect to become a successful life coach, a world renowned boxer, or a multi-millionaire overnight. Each time you plant your seeds, it is going to take time for them to flourish. You must learn to truly enjoy the entire process. Learn to rejoice in even the small victories. I get SO thankful and excited anytime I have even one sale, someone sends me a message saying I have inspired them, or I reflect on how far I have come. Yes, that is right; I do not take any growth in my business or personal life for granted. You must find the positive and the joy in the small growth along the way. This will keep you grounded, excited and passionate throughout your journey.

You cannot rush your preparation season. You cannot rush what God is doing inside of you. You are being prepared and once the right time comes, you will be ready to receive it. Sometimes if you receive what you desire at a time when you think you are ready, then you will mess up the entire thing, simply because you are not quite prepared yet. Just like a baby takes nine months to grow and fully develop in the mother's womb, your dream will take time to develop, too. Your baby, your dream, is growing inside of you. At the right time, when your maturing season ends, you will give birth. In the meantime, keep nurturing and investing in your dream, even when it seems like you are working in vain. You cannot see the baby inside the womb, but that baby is in there growing and preparing to be exposed to the world.

Remind yourself that you are pregnant with purpose and will give birth in due season whenever you find yourself getting discouraged. I personally have wanted to give up SO many times but I am willing to fight for what I want. I am determined to punch discouragement, anxiety, worry, stress and fear in the face every day in order to grow and continue to bloom into the person God created me to be. I refuse to live a life of mediocrity. I will keep pushing even when it seems nothing is happening because I understand that I will reap what I have sown.

Each day find something that you can learn from on your journey and remember that you are inspiring someone else to keep going, too. Your story is a book, a lecture, or a testimony away from changing someone else's life and your own. Do not give up in your "grind it out, hard work" season. Do not look for an instant victory. Make up your mind to be in it to win it even if it takes longer than you anticipated. Life is a journey of ups and downs. Sometimes you will win and sometimes things will not go your way, but you will learn from the experience.

The people that you think have such an awesome life are able to live that way now because they did not give up, they kept their eyes on how far they have come, they chose to find joy along the way, they celebrated even the smallest victories, and they continued when the going got tough! Do not compare your life, be envious, or try to compete with anyone else; just keep running your own race. Keep your eyes on your own journey and trust that you can win, too! It is now up to you to make a daily decision to fight for the future life you desire and deserve!

As the Bible tells us in Hebrews 11:11, the beautiful thing about faith is, "Now faith is the substance of things hoped for, the evidence of things not seen." This scripture is a great reminder that although we may not have all the answers, we must still step out and try what we believe the Lord has placed on our hearts to do. You will not have a step-by-step guide when you first start out but I believe wholeheartedly that you will be led by God when you follow the call He has placed on your heart. Challenge yourself to go after that dream even if you are trembling in fear. Once you do it, you will realize that you had nothing to fear in the first place. It is crazy how taking a leap of faith can make you bold and teach you how to overcome the things that you once feared.

You cannot entertain fear and faith at the same time, so you must choose one. You cannot keep telling yourself that what you believe is not possible and magically expect it to manifest in your life. In the Bible, James 2:14 reads, "What does it profit, my brethren, if someone says he has faith but does not have works? Can faith save him?" This scripture is a gentle reminder that you must put some action behind that goal. You cannot be idle and expect doors to open for you. Walking by faith requires action but can send you places and open doors that you could not even imagine. An indescribable joy lies on the inside of you when you know that you are walking in your calling, or your purpose, and you are truly changing lives. This happens when you stop allowing your fearful emotions to push you around and you decide that you are going to at least challenge yourself to try, frightened or not.

If you stay consistent and continue exercising that faith muscle, then eventually you will start seeing some positive results and that will motivate you to keep going. God will be right by your side and will not abandon you during your faith-walking journey. I love Deuteronomy 31:6. It reads, "Be strong and courageous. Do not be afraid or terrified because of them, for the LORD your God goes with you; he will never leave you nor forsake you." This scripture is such a beautiful reminder that you are never alone. God is always there even in the midst of life's greatest challenges. He will never leave your side. Remain obedient, constantly pray for wisdom, and trust that the Lord is leading you every step of the way. Now challenge yourself to get started today.

Once you take that leap of faith and finally get started, prepare yourself to practice having good ol' patience. We live in a microwave society. We have instant popcorn, instant toaster pastries, instant technology, and almost instant everything. This has caused humans to expect quick and easy results. I am guilty as charged with this one. I am not the most patient person and this is an area in which I am constantly growing. I like to see results right away (don't we all). Sometimes I have to tell myself, "Sit your little impatient tail down and trust God's timing for your life." I might even think, *I'm sowing this seed, I'm watering it, and I don't see any harvest. What's up with that?* I am human, so I become frustrated at times. However, I remind myself that nothing great comes easy. It is important to continue doing the work regardless of the results that you currently see. This is why being passionate about what you do is important; you will have moments where you get tested, things will seem like they are at a standstill, and you will want to give up.

My patience has grown SO much, especially with growing a health company. Everything does not always go my way, people do not always support what I am doing, and sometimes business deals do not work out. I tell myself constantly that, in God's perfect timing, everything will work out just the way He intended. We must all continue to believe and walk by faith and not by what our physical eyes see. Even this book was just a vision at one point in time. It took time to write it, edit it, create a book cover design, and publish it but now in the right timing, it has been birthed, printed and distributed. Now you are reading it.

Timing and patience is everything. If I would have stopped writing because it was taking months to finish, then I would have aborted the process due to impatience, which would have caused me to get in my own way and not be able to share valuable wisdom with you. Your purpose is not just for you. The path you take will be a blessing to others because someone else needs the knowledge you have. So do not abort your purpose just because it is taking longer than you expected. It is better to enjoy the journey, so stop putting a time limit on everything and keep making progress. As you continue to put one foot in front of the other, one day you will look up, and this beautiful path will be right in front of you.

Remind yourself that just like going to the gym, you cannot go for two days and expect to win the "fit body of the year" award. You must continue to go to the gym, build your muscle and be dedicated to the process. Then, you will eventually see some amazing results. When I decided to compete in pageants, I had to keep trying every time I did not win. I had to keep working out, keep practicing my interview skills, and keep practicing my walk even when I was not getting the results I desired. I was consistent and willing to work hard for the pageant titles I did win. When I finally won, it made the victory that much sweeter because I actually invested in myself and worked my tail off, and it eventually came together for me.

I know that nothing is going to be given to me, so although I have been impatient while growing a company, while competing in pageants, and while being rejected for certain jobs, I was not going to let any of that stop me. Did I feel discouraged sometimes? I would be lying if I said no. I felt upset many times but I decided to stick to my vision and goals. Therefore, if you find yourself in an impatient state of mind right now, allow your mind to rest, or even take a break if you need to, but do not stop planting. In due time God will open the right doors of favor just for you!

CHAPTER 6

꙳

Rest in God's Promises and Face Your Fears

The unknown zone is SCARY! It does not feel good when you have no clue what to do next, no sign of the next turn, or no idea how to get the funds to birth your dream. You might ask the following questions: Who's going to support me? What if I look stupid? What if it doesn't work out? What if I fail? My response is, it is okay if it does not work out. At least you tried. At least you are figuring it out. That is what truly matters. You are trying, learning and growing along the way. Remember, success is a process.

Do not entertain those silly thoughts trying to keep you stuck in your comfort zone. You birth beauty outside of your comfort zone. You must fight back and punch those thoughts of doubt in the face by facing your fears head on. I literally had to condition my mind and tell myself, "I don't care if I feel afraid; I'm doing it anyway. Oh, those people aren't cheering for me? SO WHAT? I will not let that stop me. I will cheer for myself." If a plan did not work out for me, then my response was, "Okay, not everything is going to go exactly as I planned. It's a lesson learned and I will use it to draft a better plan next time."

You see, it is all about changing your perspective. This journey is a learning experience and fear is nothing more than lies being planted in your head from the enemy. He wants to keep you stuck, and you must refuse to entertain his lies. When your mind attempts to convince you of all the reasons why you cannot do something, you must take control and fight back. This is when you speak life and tell yourself how creative and talented you are. You tell yourself that God created you on purpose, with purpose, and you will not live your life crippled in fear. I urge you to start now with what you have. If you are a makeup artist and all you have is a cell phone to snap pictures of your work, then that is perfectly fine. Start uploading your pictures to social media. You do not need a professional camera to get started. The key is to get started and to build some momentum by putting action behind your plan, working at it day-by-day.

Over time you will start to see some progress. I encourage you to let those fearful emotions fuel you to go after the life you desire. Remind yourself that feeling afraid is normal when you step into something new. Every person who has ever accomplished something great experienced fear at first. The difference between a successful person and a non-successful person is the choices they make. The successful person feels afraid but pursues their dream anyway. When times are tough, they keep going. The unsuccessful person decides to let fear stop them. They decide to take the safe route.

Every time you decide to take fear head on, you grow one step closer to your goal and you become more fearless. Defeating the fear within will become easier for you each time you decide to face it head on regardless of how afraid you are. You must choose to travel the unknown path to discover where it leads you. Most people do not succeed because they are not willing to try. Tomorrow is not promised, so why not start today? If you want to live a fulfilled, purposeful life, then you must do it NOW. Do it afraid; I guarantee your results will eventually shock you.

Your human emotions can influence you to make permanent decisions based off of temporary feelings. If you are not cautious of your fickle emotions, then they will try to control you. I have to tell myself how to feel DAILY because it is easy to slip into "worry land", "frustrated land", and "I have to figure this out land". I have had so many moments of "how will this work out", "what route should I take", "what's going to happen next", "why did this happen", and so on. I have learned and consistently must practice how to choose my thoughts on purpose instead of pondering on every thought that arises in my mind.

Naturally, as humans, we want to know how every little detail will work out in our lives. When we do not understand how something will turn out, our minds will instantly drift into finding a solution. We have a natural tendency to try to figure out every situation. Yet, you must remember not to allow anything that you cannot control to crowd your mental space or consume your thoughts. I know it is not easy to do, but you must learn to trust that the God who created you is the same God that will lead you, provide for you, heal you, restore you, and give you the wisdom you seek. Rest in the peace of the Lord when you find yourself anxious over a situation that you cannot seem to map out.

I love Philippians 4:7: "And the peace of God, which surpasses all understanding, will guard your hearts and your minds in Christ Jesus." That verse reminds me to find peace in the midst of whatever I am going through. It reminds me that God will take care of me and He understands exactly what I am going through. When you feel yourself becoming overwhelmed, step away and give yourself some time to free your mind. You do not always need to have every single detail figured out.

Shut down the habit of worrying immediately or before you know it, you will be sad, stressed out and depressed, and you will feel like giving up on your journey completely. Living the life you desire and going after your dream is NOT going to be easy. To be honest with you, at times it is HARD! It does not always feel good and you will have MANY moments where you want to just quit and run away from it all. In these uncomfortable moments, you will have to decide to take control of your thinking and to not rely on your emotions. You will have to cast down the fear, anxiety, and all the worrisome thoughts.

Worry can appear similar to a parasite that eats away at you and makes you mentally and physically sick. Studies have shown that chronic worrying leads to high anxiety. This can cause you to experience a loss of appetite, sleep, and also lead to health problems. Excessive stress causes your body to go into fight or flight, which causes your nervous system to release stress hormones. This can lead to dizziness, headaches, irregular heartbeat, rapid breathing, muscle tension, depression, suicidal thoughts, and shortness of breath. If you habitually ponder on the wrong things, and do not consciously choose your thoughts, then it will negatively affect your life.

You must rest your mind, relax, seek professional help if needed, and trust that what's meant to be will work itself out. If you know in your heart that God placed you on a specific path, then you must keep going regardless of how hard it gets. God will lead you and provide you with strength along the way. If you find yourself in a state of worry, then decide to let it go. Become relentless in the pursuit of your dreams, regardless of how you feel.

Let me be clear, I do not want to make it seem as if you will never feel yourself in a state of panic where your emotions run high, because you will. The goal is to take control and to not fret or allow your fickle emotions to control you. Choose to find joy in the midst of figuring it out. Most times when I find myself worrying, I waste a ton of energy worrying in vain because the situation always works out. Now I tell myself to trust that everything will work out how it is supposed to. I am human, but I try hard to control my mind and to not allow worry to consume me. This is a friendly reminder to take control of your mental health, choose to no longer frustrate yourself, and trust that everything will come together for you in due time!

When things are not going so well and you begin to feel overwhelmed, take time to slip away to your quiet place and to remind yourself, "It's only a temporary season that I must endure and it WILL come to an end." Do not allow your broken, hard seasons to defeat you. Do not allow your emotions to control you. Those rough seasons are the building blocks for your future. Those bumps in the road will prepare you for the future. When you are facing tough moments, try hard to focus on the good. You are growing, you are becoming stronger, you are learning, and you are becoming a better person. You can even use your testimony to bless others one day. Just know that no matter what you are facing, you are strong enough to handle it.

God's word tells us in Ecclesiastes 3:1, "There is a time for everything, and a season for every activity under the heavens." This verse is a kind reminder that NOTHING lasts forever, circumstances will change, and seasons come and go. Regardless of where you currently find yourself, remember that change is coming if you just keep moving forward. Even if it seems as if things will never change, trust that change will eventually come.

Life can consist of moments where it seems like you are going to be stuck in a difficult season forever. I am here to remind and encourage you that you will not. Keep doing what you can and keep trusting that you are going to come out of your hardship victorious. If you are currently in a beautiful, happy season, then do not take it for granted. Cherish every moment because life can change in the blink of an eye. I also want to remind you to soak up every opportunity that comes your way. Do not take any door of favor for granted because those seasons also change. Learn to embrace the open doors and to hang on in the challenging times. You've got this!

Life flows better when you CHOOSE to have a grateful heart. Focusing on the negative things, or the things that make you feel sad, will not help you. That kind of thinking is detrimental and will only hurt you. It hinders your growth, your progress, your mindset and your life. Whatever you place your focus on will be magnified in your life, so you must find the good and give thanks for that!

I know at times you might think, "Ugh, my life stinks! Why couldn't I have a fairy tale existence, and why must life be so difficult?" The truth is, we all face rough seasons, even the most successful people that you see and admire. They have learned how to successfully control their daily habits and habitual thought patterns. Successful people choose to shift their focus when a negative thought surfaces in their mind. They choose to find a better thought to ponder on that will be beneficial to them instead of a hindrance.

I challenge you to take the next twenty-four hours to consciously watch your thinking patterns. When you catch a negative thought, switch it to something that you are grateful for within twenty seconds. You might think that you do not have anything to be thankful for at this point in your life. Yes you do! You are alive right now. Many people took their last breath yesterday and would do anything to have another day to fulfill their purpose on this earth. You have been given another day to try again, to create better daily habits, to take control of your mind, and to create a better future for yourself and for those around you.

If you woke up in your right mind, and you have all five senses, food to eat, clothes on your back, a house to live in, family who loves you, money to pay your bills, friends that are there for you, a car to drive, and clean water to drink, then you are BLESSED! You must be grateful for every blessing, even the things that may seem insignificant, and choose to give thanks. Someone somewhere is living on the street, dealing with addiction, selling their body for money, cannot wash their own body, cannot see, without a car, without a job, without any food, and may no longer have their limbs. However, some of those people still manage to find joy! Some of those people would love to have the life you now complain about; they would take it without a complaint.

At times we all must step away and truly dissect our lives, our blessings, and just how good GOD really is to each and every one of us. Choose today to find joy in the midst of any storm that you might currently face. Know that just like you came out of the last storm with strength, you will come out of this one or any future storm as well. Do not allow life to discourage you to the point where you lose hope. Things will get better for you. Find the good in your life, discover the things that make you happy, and constantly dwell on them!

CHAPTER 7

⋘⋙

Excuses Will Steal Your Destiny

We all have been guilty of making excuses to justify why something happened the way it did, or to defend our behavior even though it was wrong. You might be familiar with excuses like, "I can't work out; I'm too tired but I still want a six-pack," or "I was late because I kept pressing snooze on my alarm clock, but I still want to get promoted without putting in the effort." It is easy to allow excuses to become your scapegoat when you are simply unsure, you made a mistake, you do not want to look bad, or you feel uneasy about what to do. People also use excuses to place the blame on others when they do not want to accept responsibility or to face the truth.

Many times we make excuses without realizing they keep us from our destiny. They hold us back, yet we cling to them so tightly. Your excuses are bad habits that must be broken in order to truly face your future and to make your dreams a reality. You will not be able to make an excuse for why your donut shop sales have decreased when you chose to use a cheaper dough that changed the taste of the donuts. You will not be able to make an excuse for why your organization is not growing because you are not invested in finding ways to make it flourish. If you want to see change, then YOU must change. You cannot continue to do the same thing over and over and hope for a different outcome.

If you know you are the king or queen of excuses, then this chapter will challenge you to change in that area. The next time something happens that was totally in your control, instead of making excuses and shifting the blame, decide within yourself to take full responsibility. You must face the reality of the circumstances you created in order to make positive changes within yourself and your future endeavors. In order to reach your full potential, you must stop finding an excuse for every little thing. Analyze your life right now and determine if you are pleased with where you are. If the answer is no, then ask yourself if you have been making excuses that are possibly holding you back from pursuing the life you desire. If you are willing to be honest with yourself, then let go of the excuses that hold you back. When you live your life with integrity and face your fears head on, things will eventually work out for you!

I know this is easier said than done, especially when fearful thoughts are attacking your mind. It is hard to not be controlled by those thoughts. It is easy to let fear bully you into thinking that you cannot pursue your dream. One of the biggest fears that tends to stop people from trying something new is the fear of judgement. Some people would rather not try, and then make an excuse that they are waiting on the right timing, waiting until they have enough cash, or just waiting until they feel more prepared. All of these excuses hinder your progress. Your future is counting on you to make a move in a different direction, regardless of what other people may think.

People's opinions of you are not your business and should not take any of your focus away from chasing after the dream God placed on your heart. If you want to accomplish anything, then you truly have to take that leap and face the fear of what other people might think of you. Some people will have something to say regardless of whether you try or not, so why not just go for it? You have to let people think what they want to think and place your focus on what you can control, which involves doing what is best for you.

Another fear that causes some people to make excuses is the fear of failure. The fear of what if you give it your all, invest your money and go all out but it still does not work out. It is okay if you try and it does not go exactly as planned. Some of the ideas that I have tried did not go as good as I thought they would, or did not get the response that I anticipated, but I did not let that stop me. I have gained valuable knowledge from everything that did not work out and it is helping me change and grow in a better way. When you take your first leap of faith, place your focus on creating, building and learning. This will help you enjoy the journey more and not put so much pressure on yourself to get immediate results.

If you are able to place your focus on giving the journey your all, then this will ease the fear of failure. You will have a contentment that you gave it everything you had and despite what the outcome may be, you can be thankful for the growth and the experience instead of the pressure to accomplish some major results right away. Remember, you are learning and you will be more prepared for the next leap of faith that you take. It is a journey and it is not always going to work out. It is normal to feel fear as well, but do not let that fear cause you to make excuses that will stop you from at least trying. If you never try, then how will you know what would or could have happened? It is time to let go of the excuses that are holding you back from your future. Go after it!

Another potential threat to your progress is procrastination, which shares a close relationship with excuses. It will creep up on you and before you know it, three years will have passed and you still will not have started your dance company, written your book, launched your t-shirt company, or whatever your goal may be. It is SO easy to put off what should be done today until tomorrow, then tomorrow becomes next month, until you wake up one day living in regret. Time is something that you can never get back. Time is such a precious gift from the Lord and it should not be taken for granted. Do not grow old without at least trying to use your gifts and going after your dreams. You must be determined to give life all you have. You do not want to look back twenty-five years from now and say to yourself, "I sure wish I would have traveled more, built that organization, or launched my clothing line." You want to grow old knowing that you gave life your best shot.

You have one life to live and right now is the time to start living it. Ask yourself what do you really want to accomplish in your life. What do you feel led to do? Now ask yourself what is stopping you. Write down all three responses and then make an action plan to start right away. List the steps that you plan to take to get your vision from your mind to a physical step-by-step to do list. Do not worry if you do not have all the answers. I did not have all the answers when I launched my health company Be A Health Nut Too. I simply took the first step by launching a health blog and trusted God to lead me. I never would have expected that six months after launching my blog, I would be invited on a health tour to speak in the country, England, and the states Georgia and Michigan, along with a few other states. I did not know that I would be asked to film two health documentaries, *The Full Body Detox* and *Urban Kryptonite*. I had no clue that my health blog would eventually turn into a health company where I am now able to make all natural plant-based products and ship them worldwide. Be A Health Nut Too products are also now offered in a few local health stores. I am still in awe of the extent of God's favor when you learn to be obedient. It amazes me to think of the doors that can open when you simply try. It was never my plan to start a health company; I simply followed what the Holy Spirit led me to do, and now I have a small business. I give all glory to God and I am thankful that I listened even when I felt afraid.

Sometimes it just takes blind faith, it takes jumping, and it takes walking into what seems to be uncomfortable for your path and purpose to unfold. Now it is your turn to step out and try. You must trust that the answers will come as you go. You might say, "I don't even know where to start." That is completely fine. I suggest that you start by writing out what you desire, pray for guidance, listen to inspirational speakers, and study those individuals that have done what you would like to do. As you begin to learn from their stories, ideas will come. It is also great to find a mentor that can potentially guide you, someone who has accomplished the results you are looking to accomplish. You are going to want to invest in your personal growth by any means necessary!

I want you to view procrastination as your enemy. It is trying to stop you, and you must defeat it by taking action! Do the very thing that you have been afraid to do. Wake up every day and keep putting one foot in front of the other and trust that God will lead your path.

Now let's discuss another area that I like to call "the distractions of life". Distractions can be a major problem as you pursue your goals. It is so easy to be distracted if you are not mindful of who and what you are giving your attention to. This world is flooded with messages, images, commercials, news, reality television, people, music, and social media platforms all seeking to capture your attention. Some of those distractions will corrupt your mind and make you act upon what you see. Some companies pay marketing agencies to make seducing advertisements for them in order to manipulate your mind and make you crave what they are trying to sell you.

For instance, I know that you might think music is not trying to control you or to sell you something. However, I challenge you to listen carefully to the lyrics of many of the mainstream songs and pay attention to how you feel and act when listening to certain types of music. Music, television, social media, and the people you hang around most can and will influence you if you are not consciously aware of the subliminal messages being pumped into your mind.

Have you ever caught yourself repeating your friend's favorite catch phrase, or heard yourself humming a song after you heard it a few hours ago? This is because those messages have penetrated your heart and now you are repeating or singing what you heard. Now this can be a good or bad thing depending on what influences you. Make sure that you are not allowing the wrong seeds to be planted inside your heart. You must guard yourself from the negative things and people to which you expose your heart and mind. I've had to unfriend numerous people on my social media accounts for posting things that I did not want to see or have fed into my spirit. It is nothing personal, but when you are working on becoming the best version of yourself, you are not going to be able to hang with just any and everybody.

Some people are comfortable living a life that influences them to do things that will harm them in the future. It is not a judgement against them; I just choose to make decisions now that will benefit my life in the future. I refuse to allow any distraction to uproot the good that I have been planting inside of my heart. It is your life, so do not feel bad for choosing to surround yourself with the best people and ridding your life of any and everything that will potentially harm you. You are the boss of your life and it is okay to upgrade your relationships. I do not even watch television. I have chosen to not allow the fear pumping messages from the news, or the messy drama of reality television shows to run rampant inside of my mind. No thanks! I am aware of what is going on in the world around me, but I am not consumed by it.

Social media has also become a major distraction for many people. While it is a great way to connect with so many wonderful people, it can become a source of wasting precious time that you can never get back. I know people that spend hours just browsing the newsfeed, getting engulfed in other people's drama, comparing their lives to the highlight reels of others, then feeling bad about themselves. Do any of these examples describe you? If so, then it is time to make a change. Your time is too valuable to spend it being distracted by an online social media feed. Make a list of everything and everyone in your life that possibly distracts you. Then make a list of how you can distance yourself from the things that are currently not beneficial to you and your growth. Today is the perfect day to take control of your life and to cut off the things and people that are not helping to push you closer to living the life you desire. You can be either distracted or focused but you cannot do both at the same time. It is important to use your time wisely; it is the one thing that you can never get back.

CHAPTER 8

❧

Invest In Yourself and Impact the World

You have started your company, your blog, your organization, and now it is time to build your brand. How exciting! The question is, how in the world do you get the right people to discover your brand? Fortunately, we have been blessed with social media, which can reach millions of people when used correctly. I struggled with this area when I first started Be A Health Nut Too. I was building a following of people that were not necessarily my target audience. You live and you learn, right? You cannot promote donuts to someone interested in buying paint. It is not that the painting crew does not like your donuts but they are interested paint, which is a totally different genre.

You must find people that actually need the service your company, organization or brand offers. You can have ten thousand followers but if they are not true supporters, then you are not going to receive the response and support that you desire. It is not that people are being mean, but maybe you just need to discover your niche market. Not everyone is your target audience. You cannot make everyone happy, and not everyone is going to support you. Do not place your focus on who supports you but focus on getting your brand to the right people. Before you know it, you will have some loyal supporters that will come to every event you have, purchase every book or product, and tell others about your brand. Once you find the right people and build trust with each of them, they will naturally support you!

After identifying your target audience, discover which social media platforms fit your brand best and learn how to use them effectively. I like Facebook and Instagram but I also use Twitter. When you post on whichever forum you choose, be sure to study what your followers respond to, pay attention to what pictures get the most interactions, and look at your analytics. This will help you figure out what is valuable and useful to share. Remember this is not about you, what you like, or what you think is great content; it is about what your customers and clients value and find interesting. Think from their perspective, put yourself in their shoes, and not your own. What problems are your customers having that you can currently solve? Place yourself in that mindset and your brand will eventually grow.

Make sure that what you post represents you and is not damaging to your brand. I recommend not sharing your personal life on your business page. I would suggest keeping your personal life completely separate from your business page. Your business page is where you share products, events, books, inspiration, and future promotional posts. Your potential customers do not need to know your family drama, marital issues, what you were doing last night, or anything of that nature. Now if you are looking to share your life by way of vlogging and becoming a public influencer where you are the brand, then by all means you can share your daily life, but I still would suggest not sharing drama-filled content. You want to build a reputable brand that someday an investor may want to buy, so always think before you post. Going viral is not always worth it!

Create a hashtag that is special to your brand and use it every time you post. This will link all of your posts together and allow others to share your content using your special hashtag. Anytime I post, I always hashtag #BeAHealthNutToo which now has all my content in one place. Also, find some of the most popular hashtags that represent your brand and use those when you share a new image as well. Hashtags are great because they allow new potential followers to find your page and to follow you. Another great way to build your following is to find other accounts similar to yours and to engage with their content. Please do not do this in a spammy kind of way. When you like or comment on their post in a genuine fashion, it potentially allows new eyes to see your comment, to visit your page, and to follow you.

You also can do shout for shouts with brands similar to yours. I would not suggest doing this often but once every few months is perfectly fine. When you do a shout for shout, you will share your fellow colleague's photo and tell people to follow their page and they will do the same. This helps their followers discover your brand and helps you build your following quicker as well.

If you can get your products, your brand and your organization into the hands of influencers, then this can truly change the credibility of your brand overnight. Just like big companies like Nike use celebrities to market their shoes, finding influencers that are connected to the target audience that you want to connect with can help grow your brand and give it instant credibility by simply having an influencer share your products, book or company.

If you are just starting out with only five hundred followers and you are able to get someone with two million followers to share your content, then this opportunity will expand your brand quicker than years of marketing would. Search for people that are in the same industry as you, and that have a large following, and send an email to see if you can work out a special promotional deal with them. You can also email them to see if you can simply send them a gift package with your materials and they just might share it. It does not hurt to try and could truly help change your company. Think outside the box and seek ways to market your business that may not be the norm. Find some influencers and do not be afraid to reach out to them.

When you start your social media pages, be sure to post consistent material. If you start off sharing fashion, then continue to post fashion based content. You must remember that you are building trust with people, and if you want to become an expert in your field, then staying consistent with what you share is one great way to do that. People will support those that they trust. If your followers feel like they can trust what you say because you have remained consistent, then they will be more willing to act when you need them to. If one day you are sharing fashion, the next day you are sharing how to make a baby roll over, and the next week you are sharing how to rebuild a torn down school, then your message might become confusing to your followers. I have stayed consistent with my health, wellness, and inspirational brand messaging and it has helped my company continue to grow.

You also want to make sure that your images look nice. Do not just post some sloppy, barely thought out picture on your pages. You must remember that everything you post represents you and your company. Post things that you would be okay with showing years from now. So let's say your brand will be based on living plants. You do not want to share an image of a plant right next to a dirty laundry basket. Instead, set the plant in a place with a nice background or a plain backdrop and take a nice image. It does not need to be extra fancy, but make it look as neat and professional as possible. Once you figure out what your brand will be, post about it at least three to four times a week, stick to your topic, and eventually your consistency will pay off.

Word of mouth is the best marketing any company or brand can use. When others praise your products, or tell someone else how your book, coaching course, or event changed their life, it is the best form of promotion.

Whenever a person shares a positive review about your company or product, be sure to repost that review. This builds your brand credibility. You want to show your customers, clients and network that you appreciate their support, so shout them out and show them love. Respond to questions, feedback, and actually interact with your audience. While online interaction differs from in person interaction, you are still building a relationship with your followers. People do not have to support you, so be VERY grateful when they do.

If you really want to change your life, then you MUST be willing to invest in yourself, your journey, your brand and your knowledge. One of the best things I have done is buy books, listen to webinars, attend live seminars, and put that knowledge to great use. The more you know, the more you will grow. I am able to help many people now because of the work that I have been doing on myself behind the scenes for years. I am not the same person that I was five years ago because I have taken the time to put myself in personal development school in order to grow and become the best version of myself.

If you do not know how to do something, then someone out there does, and it is up to you to seek that information and to apply it to your own life. If you cannot afford to pay for a live seminar, then there is an abundance of FREE information available at the click of a button. Use YouTube and search for videos on how to accomplish what you want to achieve.

Find cooking, makeup, business or fashion courses, or whatever you believe your purpose is, and study those areas. You have heard the saying, "If you don't believe in you, no one will", well the same applies to investing. If you are not willing to invest your own money, time and energy into your dream, then how do you expect anyone else to feel excited about investing in your dream?

I have invested SO much time, money and energy into growing Be A Health Nut Too, but it has not been an easy journey. I do not always see results right away but I know that I am doing what I feel led by God to do, and I continue to trust His plans day-by-day. I was willing to invest in my own knowledge, my company and my personal development. Now after years of studying and planting seeds, I am finally starting to see the beginning stages of my harvest. If you are willing to invest in yourself, do whatever it takes, spend your own hard earned money for your dream, and put in the work required to live a purpose-filled life, then, the right connections and doors of favor WILL eventually open for you.

If you are reading this book, then I know you are serious about changing your life. You are tired of allowing fear to defeat you and you are ready to go after the life you deserve. Now is the time to put the knowledge you have gained into action DAILY. Speak life over your vision. Cheer for yourself. Continue to invest in the knowledge needed to change your life. Connect with those that are living a life of positivity, on the right path, and those that inspire you. Keep striving for your goals and keep watering those seeds, and in due time all your hard work will pay off. I am rooting for each of you. Now go PUNCH YOUR FEAR IN THE FACE!

Action Plan: Use the next few pages of this book to write out, in as much detail as possible, a clear vision of your business, blog, organization or book and how you plan to get there. I suggest focusing on one or two goals at a time. Do not spread yourself too thin trying to do everything all at once. The more time, energy and focus you can give to your vision, the better. When you try to focus on too many things at one time, it is going to be harder to get anything accomplished. I suggest mastering one area first, letting it grow, building a strong foundation, and placing your focus there.

A few questions to answer in your action plan:

What is your two-week, one-month, three-month, six-month, and one-year plan? Who should you connect with? What problem does your business solve? How can your vision be used to bless others? What are three goals that you want to accomplish after writing out this action plan? How soon would you like to accomplish those goals? How will you market your company? Who is your target audience? Why do you want to birth this vision? What social media platforms will be most beneficial to market your brand? When times get tough, what are your five victory words that you will speak out loud to keep yourself motivated to not give up? What is your long-term goal? Where do you see yourself in five to seven years from now?

This gives you a guideline to start with. If you change things along the way, then that is completely fine but this action plan will be a good start for you. I cannot wait to hear about your success stories! Now GO get what is yours!

MY ACTION PLAN

※

_____

_____

_____

_____

_____

_____

_____

_____

_____

_____

_____

LaShana Gardner

103

PUNCH YOUR FEAR IN THE FACE

104

LaShana Gardner

_____

_____

_____

_____

_____

_____

_____

_____

_____

_____

_____

_____

_____

_____

_____